The Wiggles and friends Song & Activity Book

This book belongs to:

....

Hello Everybody!

Welcome to our very special song and activity book.
Here are eighteen songs for you to sing—plus the sheet music so your older friends
and family members can play along on the piano, keyboard and guitar.

You can be your own Wiggles band!

Every song has a game to play and fun things for you to make—
you can even create your own Big Red Car!

Invite your friends to join in the fun and they
can sing and play games with you too.
We can't wait for you to sing and dance along with us.
We hope you enjoy our song and activity book.
Happy singing and wiggling!

Anthony

Greg

Jeff

Murray

Henry the Octopus®

Captain Feathersword®

Dorothy the Dinosaur®

Wags the Dog®

The Wiggles are children's entertainers whose songs are sung and enjoyed by children across the world. In *The Wiggles and Friends Song & Activity Book* you will find eighteen of their most popular and best-loved songs. The easy-to-read top-line musical arrangements come complete with all lyrics and guitar chord boxes.

The book also contains ideas for developmentally appropriate learning experiences that will engage and delight young children. Each song has a fully illustrated instructional ideas page that relates to that song, designed especially for this songbook.

The ideas in this book were originally developed by Dr. Kathleen Warren, Ed. D, MA (Hons), LASA, FTCL, who is an early childhood adviser to The Wiggles. This book can be used with groups of children in an early childhood setting or by parents and children at home as they enjoy the songs and have fun with the activities.

Also available:
The Wiggles Christmas Song & Activity Book

All activities and games must be supervised by an adult.
Please ensure children use safety scissors at all times.

Exclusive Distributors for the USA and Canada:
Music Sales Corporation
257 Park Avenue South
New York, New York 10010 USA

All Rights Reserved.

Order No. MS04053
ISBN-10: 1.8768.7194.6
ISBN-13: 978.1.8768.7194.9

Printed in Colombia by Quebecor World
Early Childhood Consultant to The Wiggles:
Kathleen Warren - Ed. D, MA (Hons), LASA, FTCL
Cover and Book Design by Glen Hannah @ Goonga Design
Music Arrangements by The Wiggles and Dominic Lindsay
Transcriptions by Sean Peter (Autopilot Productions)
Illustrations by Adam Dal Pozzo

www.thewiggles.com

CONTENTS

Toot Toot, Chugga Chugga, Big Red Car

(Murray Cook, Jeff Fatt, Anthony Field, Greg Page)
© 1998 Wiggly Tunes Pty. Ltd.
P.O. Box 657 Bondi Junction, NSW, 1355. AUSTRALIA.
International Copyright Secured. All Rights Reserved. Used by Permission.

Chorus: Toot Toot, Chu-gga Chu-gga, Big Red Car. We'll trav-el near and we'll trav-el far

Toot Toot, Chu-gga Chu-gga, Big Red Car, we're gon-na ride the whole day long.

Verse 1: Mur-ray's in the back seat, Play-ing his gui-tar,

Mur-ray's in the back seat, of the Big Red Car.

Chorus: Toot Toot, Chu-gga Chu-gga, Big Red Car We'll trav-el near and we'll trav-el far

Toot Toot, Chu-gga Chu-gga, Big Red Car, we're gon-na ride the whole day long.

Verse 2:
Jeff is fast asleep, he's having a little rest,
We'd better wake him up, so let's all call out, "Wake Up Jeff!"

Verse 3:
Anthony is eating, he's got so much food,
He's eating apples and oranges, and fruit salad too.

Verse 4:
Greg is doing the driving, he's singing scooby doo-ah,
Greg is doing the driving, of the Big Red Car.

Make your own Big Red Car!

1. Cut off the top and bottom flaps of the cardboard box but do not throw them away.

2. From these extra parts of cardboard cut four round wheels and rectangles or squares for the windows.

Color or paint the wheels black. If you wish, you can paint the remaining box red just like the Big Red Car. Then, using glue or tape, attach the wheels and windows.

4. Depending on the size of the box, one or two children can hold their new car at waist height and "drive" it around the room singing "Toot Toot, Chugga Chugga, Big Red Car."

More Ideas!

Use a large cardboard box to play **Jack In The Box:**
One child climbs inside the box and squats out of sight.
The other children chant:
[Hayley] hides in the box
Until somebody opens the lid
One, two, three. . .OUT!
(The child jumps out on the count of three.)

Transportation Game: The teacher or other adult calls the name of some method of transportation and the children "travel" in whatever is suggested. "Car" means everyone drives an imaginary car. "Bicycle" means everyone rides an imaginary bicycle. "Plane" means everyone becomes a plane.

Wheelbarrows: One child walks on his/her hands and another child (or adult) holds his/her legs.

Dorothy The Dinosaur

(Murray Cook, Jeff Fatt, Anthony Field, Greg Page, John Field)
© 1991 Wiggly Tunes Pty. Ltd.
P.O. Box 657 Bondi Junction, NSW, 1355. AUSTRALIA.
International Copyright Secured. All Rights Reserved. Used by Permission.

Verse 1:

I was look-ing out my win-dow, late the oth-er night, she was sit-ting in the gar-den, and gave me such a fright. Eat-ing all mum's ros-es, there in the moon-light, it was Dor-o-thy the Di-no-saur.

Verse 2:

I knew that if mum saw her, she'd nev-er let her stay, a di-no-saur as big as that needs feed-ing night and day. I'd have to find a place where I could hide her a-way. Do-ro-thy the Di-no-saur.

Chorus:

Romp bomp - a - chomp! Romp bomp - a - chomp! Romp bomp - a - chomp! Romp bomp - a - chomp! Romp bomp - a - chomp! Romp bomp - a - chomp! Do - ro-thy the Di - no - saur, CHOMP! I knew

Verse 3:
I knew that she was so big, that she'd soon be found,
My mother called the dog catcher, he came around,
When he laid his eyes on her he fell to the ground.
Spoken: "Now I take it that's Dorothy the Dinosaur!"

Verse 4:
They called up the police, to take her right away,
They called up the zoo, to find a place to stay,
I said, they couldn't take her, I said no way,
That's Dorothy the Dinosaur.

Make a dinosaur puppet!

WHAT YOU NEED:
Safety scissors
Popsicle sticks
Cardboard
Markers/colored pencils
Glue

1. Cut out some cardboard dinosaur shapes and help the children color them in.

2. Glue a popsicle stick to the back of each dinosaur shape.

GLUE

3. Then the children can have their own dinosaur puppet. Encourage them to have their puppets interact by talking to each other.

More Ideas!

Dinosaur Mural:
Talk with the children about where dinosaurs lived.
Let the children paint a large mural
and have some cut-out dinosaur shapes
that they can paste onto it.

Captain Feathersword Fell Asleep On His Pirate Ship

(Murray Cook, Jeff Fatt, Anthony Field, Greg Page)
© 1998 Wiggly Tunes Pty. Ltd.
P.O. Box 657 Bondi Junction, NSW, 1355. AUSTRALIA.
International Copyright Secured. All Rights Reserved. Used by Permission.

Verse:

Cap-tain Feath-er-sword fell a-sleep on his pi-rate ship._____

Then he woke up on a farm._____ Oh my good-ness me!_____ With

roost-ers_____and ducks,_____ sing-ing_____ this song._____

Chorus:

Quack__ quack_____ quack__ quack__ quack, Cock-a-doo-dle doo,_____

Quack__ quack_____ quack__ quack__ quack, Cock-a-doo-dle doo,_____

Quack__ quack_____ quack__ a-doo-dle-y-doo._____

So

Verse 2:
So now every day when he talks,
This is what he says:
Quack, quack, quack, quack, quack,
Cock-a-doodle-doo.
He also does the farmyard dance,
And you can do it, too.

Verse 3:
Well is he a pirate or a rooster?
Well I just don't know,
Ahoy there, ahoy there, ahoy,
Cock-a-doodley there!
He also does the farmyard dance,
and you can do it, too.

Build your own pirate ship!

WHAT YOU NEED:
Styrofoam tray
Sticks (thin) for masts
Paper
Tape or glue

Ensure an adult is with you at all times when you are near water.

1. Using a styrofoam tray as the hull (bottom) of the ship, glue, tape or thread thin sticks to create masts and then attach paper sails to the masts.

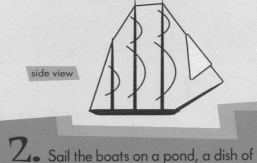

side view

2. Sail the boats on a pond, a dish of water or along some running water.

More Ideas!

Kindergarden children can come to school dressed as pirates.

_____

Sing the song "Five Little Ducks Went Out One Day."
This can be done as a finger play or it can be enacted with children playing the ducks.

_____

Make a feather collage.

_____

Visit a farm or a petting zoo.

Wake Up Jeff!

(Murray Cook, Jeff Fatt, Anthony Field, Greg Page)
© 1996 Wiggly Tunes Pty. Ltd.
P.O. Box 657 Bondi Junction, NSW, 1355. AUSTRALIA.
International Copyright Secured. All Rights Reserved. Used by Permission.

Chorus:

Wake up Jeff! Eve-ry-bod-y's wig-gling. Wake up Jeff! We real-ly need you.

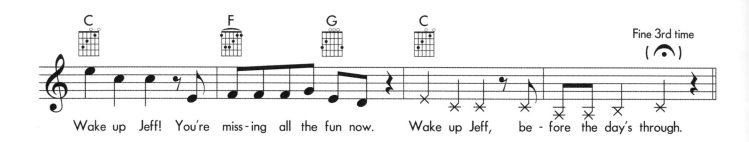

Fine 3rd time

Wake up Jeff! You're miss-ing all the fun now. Wake up Jeff, be-fore the day's through.

Verse:

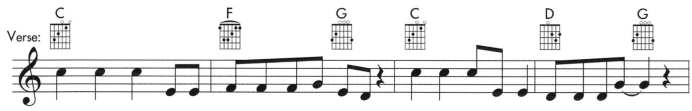

What's that sound? I can hear some-bod-y snor-ing. What's that sound? It's not Mur-ray or Greg.
Dorothy the Dino - saur is munch-ing on some ros - es. Wags the Dog, is dig-ging up bones.

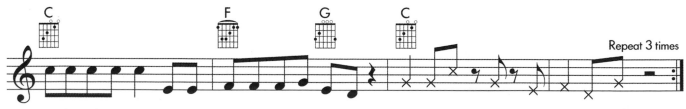

Repeat 3 times

An-tho-ny's a-wake, so let's have an-oth-er guess now. Oh, my good - ness, it must be Jeff!
Hen - ry the Oc-topus is danc-ing 'round in cir-cles. Wake up Jeff, we need you for the show!

10

Let's play Wake Up Jeff!

WHAT YOU NEED:
1 Pillow
1 Blanket
This is a game to be played with a small group of children.

1. Choose one child to be "Jeff," and the other children sit around in a circle on the floor.

2. "Jeff" lies down with a pillow and a blanket and closes their eyes.

3. All the children call out "One, two, three!" and the teacher or other adult points to one child in the circle who says, "Wake up Jeff!"

Wake up Jeff !

4. "Jeff" then "wakes up" and has to guess which child shouted "Wake up Jeff!" Another child then has a turn at being "Jeff."

More Ideas!

Children can use boxes to make beds. A big box can make a bed for a doll. Decorate the box and use pieces of material for bedding. Tea towels also make good bedding.

Mix red and blue paint together to make purple paint. Then paint a picture using only the purple paint.

Pastry Pillows. Roll out some pastry and cut into strips. Put a spoonful of filling (fruit, raisins, vegetables, meat... whatever children will like) and fold the pastry over to make little "pillows." Then bake in an oven.

We're Dancing With Wags The Dog

(Murray Cook, Jeff Fatt, Anthony Field, Greg Page)
© 1998 Wiggly Tunes Pty. Ltd.
P.O. Box 657 Bondi Junction, NSW, 1355. AUSTRALIA.
International Copyright Secured. All Rights Reserved. Used by Permission.

Let's shake our hips with Wags the Dog._____ Turn your head and groove a - long._____
Put your hands up in the air._____ Point them down once you've got them there._____
Shake your hips with Wags the Dog._____ Turn your head and groove a - long._____

Shake your hands and move your knees, we're danc - ing with Wags the Dog._____
Skip a - long like Wags would do, we're danc - ing with Wags the Dog._____
Shake your hands and move your knees, we're danc - ing with Wags the Dog._____

Ruff! Ruff Ruff! Ruff! Ruff! Now we're sing - ing it, too._____

Ruff! Ruff Ruff! Ruff! Ruff! Now Wags is dig-ging and we're all dig-ging, too._____

Now Wags is dig - ging,_____ and we're all dig - ging, too._____

12

Create a dog jigsaw puzzle!

WHAT YOU NEED:
Safety scissors
Large piece of cardboard
Large picture of a dog
Glue

1. Find a large picture of a dog and paste it onto a piece of cardboard.

2. After the glue is dry, cut the cardboard into 3-6 pieces, depending on the age of the child. Then mix up the pieces and have the children put it back together.

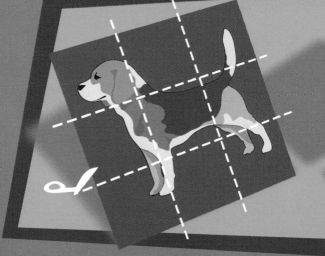

More Ideas!

Make and play a matching game. Collect some smaller dog pictures, two of each, and paste them onto cardboard squares. Children can then play a matching game. (Dog food advertisements might have some good pictures you can use.)

Who Has The Bone?

Use a bone made from cardboard or a toy bone. Blindfold one child. Give the bone to another child. The blindfolded child asks, "Who has the bone?" The child who has it says, "I've got the bone" and the child with the blindfold must guess the name of who has spoken. As an extension of this game, the child who has the bone can "bark" or say, "bow-wow." With young children, it is better to change the blindfolded child each time rather than wait for a correct guess.

Fruit Salad

(Murray Cook, Jeff Fatt, Anthony Field, Greg Page)
© 1993 Wiggly Tunes Pty. Ltd.
P.O. Box 657 Bondi Junction, NSW, 1355. AUSTRALIA.
International Copyright Secured. All Rights Reserved. Used by Permission.

14

Preparing yummy fruit salad!

WHAT YOU NEED:
Many different fruits
Chopping board
1 Knife
Large bowl

1. Collect a wide variety of fruits that you want to be in your Yummy Fruit Salad! Some ideas are: apples, bananas, oranges, grapes, pears, peaches, nectarines, plums, different types of melons.

2. Using a knife and chopping board, the adult cuts the fruit into bite-size pieces and places all the fruit salad into a large bowl. Then everyone can enjoy their Yummy Fruit Salad!

More Ideas!

Play the traditional children's game: **Oranges & Lemons**.

Make orange and lemon juice.

Talk about ripe and unripe fruit and show examples of each. Let the children decide how you can tell if fruit is ripe and ready to eat.

Go to a supermarket and see how many different varieties of fruit are on sale.

Find pictures of fruit and make a collage of those pictures.

Make fruit smoothies by blending soft fruit, milk and yogurt.

Crunchy Munchy Honey Cakes

(Murray Cook, Jeff Fatt, Anthony Field, Greg Page)
© 1994 Wiggly Tunes Pty. Ltd.
P.O. Box 657 Bondi Junction, NSW, 1355. AUSTRALIA.
International Copyright Secured. All Rights Reserved. Used by Permission.

Make cardboard bees!

WHAT YOU NEED:
Toilet paper rolls
Yellow or black paint or
crepe paper
Safety scissors
Glue or tape

1. Paint the toilet paper rolls yellow and black or wind yellow and black crepe paper around them so they look like the bee's body.

2. Cut out paper wings and attach to the "bodies" with glue or tape.

More Ideas!

Make the honey cakes following the recipe in the song.

Here Is The Beehive: This is a finger play but it can also be enacted with children being the bees. The children huddle together when they are in the hive and then "buzz" around the room when the rhyme says:
Here is the beehive, where are the bees?
Hidden away where nobody sees.
Here they come flying out of the hive,
One, two, three, four, five!

Talk about bees and honey.

Watch bees in the garden as they go to the flowers.

Who Stole The Cookie From The Cookie Jar?
In this old favorite, children sit in a circle and clap or tap to the rhythm of the rhyme:

Teacher begins:	*Who stole the cookie from the cookie jar?*
	Joe stole the cookie from the cookie jar.
Joe says:	*Who me.*
Group & Teacher:	*Yes you.*
Joe:	*Not me!*
Group & Teacher:	*Then who?*
Joe says another child's name:	*Alex!*
Everyone:	*Who stole the cookie from the cookie jar?*
	Alex stole the cookie from the cookie jar.
...and so on...	

Hot Potato

(Murray Cook, Jeff Fatt, Anthony Field, Greg Page, John Field)
© 1994 Wiggly Tunes Pty. Ltd.
P.O. Box 657 Bondi Junction, NSW, 1355. AUSTRALIA.
International Copyright Secured. All Rights Reserved. Used by Permission.

Chorus:

Hot po-ta-to hot po-ta-to,
Cold spa-ghet-ti cold spa-ghet-ti,
response on repeat: (cold spaghetti cold spaghetti)

Hot po-ta-to hot po-ta-to,
Cold spa-ghet-ti cold spa-ghet-ti,
(cold spaghetti cold spaghetti)

Hot po-ta-to hot po-ta-to,
Cold spa-ghet-ti cold spa-ghet-ti,
(spaghetti)

po-ta-to,
spa-ghet-ti,
(spaghetti)

po-ta-to po-ta-to po-ta-to.___
spa-ghet-ti, spa-ghet-ti spa-ghet-ti.___

"pop" Ooh wig-gy wig-gy wig-gy, Ooh wig-gy wig-gy wig-gy, Gim-me that gim-me that gim-me that food.___

Ooh wig-gy wig-gy wig-gy, Ooh wig-gy wig-gy wig-gy, Gim-me that gim-me that food. Mashed ba-na-na mashed ba-

Chorus:

Hot po-ta-to hot po-

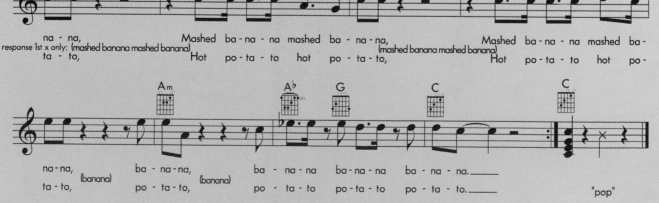

na-na, Mashed ba-na-na mashed ba-na-na, Mashed ba-na-na mashed ba-
response 1st x only: (mashed banana mashed banana)   (mashed banana mashed banana)
ta-to, Hot po-ta-to hot po-ta-to, Hot po-ta-to hot po-

na-na, ba-na-na, ba-na-na ba-na-na ba-na-na.___
(banana) (banana)
ta-to, po-ta-to, po-ta-to po-ta-to po-ta-to.___
"pop"

Making potato prints

WHAT YOU NEED:
A few raw potatoes
1 Knife
Metal spoons
Paint
Large sheet(s) of paper
1 Plate or shallow bowl

1. Wash raw potatoes thoroughly and let dry.

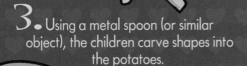

2. Using a knife, the adult cuts the potatoes in half.

3. Using a metal spoon (or similar object), the children carve shapes into the potatoes.

4. Pour some paint into a shallow plate, bowl, or dish. Dip the carved potatoes in the paint and make prints by pushing the shapes onto the paper.

More Ideas!

Cook potatoes - boil and mash them or bake in the oven.
___

Plant seed potatoes or cut the eyes out of potatoes and plant them.
___

Make potato puppets and enact scenes between two or three puppets. Use sticks for arms and legs and buttons or other such objects for eyes, nose, and mouth. The scenes can be satisfying to children if an adult takes one role. He/She can ask questions that can challenge the children such as, "Mrs. Potato, where did you grow?" or "What can you see with all your eyes?" Questions that encourage children to predict, hypothesize, explain and speculate.
___

Have a spoon and potato race. The race need not be competitive.
___

Make a spaghetti collage (or use other pasta).
___

Paint and thread pasta onto string.

Head, Shoulders, Knees & Toes

(Traditional. Arranged by Murray Cook, Jeff Fatt, Anthony Field, Greg Page)
© 1998 Wiggly Tunes Pty. Ltd.
P.O. Box 657 Bondi Junction, NSW, 1355. AUSTRALIA.
International Copyright Secured. All Rights Reserved. Used by Permission.

Intro:

Verse 1 & 6: Head, shoul-ders, knees and toes, knees and toes.   Head, shoul-ders, knees and

2: _____

3: _____

4: _____

5: _____

toes, knees and toes___ and eyes, and ears, and mouth___ and nose.   Head,   shoul-ders, knees and

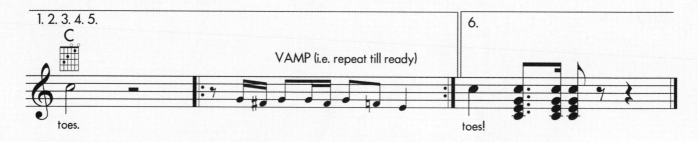

1. 2. 3. 4. 5.

VAMP (i.e. repeat till ready)

6.

toes.   toes!

Spoken during VAMP section before each verse:

2. All right, this time we're not going to sing "Head." We're just going to point to it without saying anything. Here we go...

3. Now this time we're not going to say "Head" or "Shoulders." We're just going to point to our head and shoulders. Here we go...

4. Now this time we're not going to say "Head," " Shoulders" or "Knees." We're just going to point to those three things. Here we go...

5. Now this time we're not going to say "Head." We're not going to say "Shoulders." We're not going to say "Knees,"
   and we're not going to say "Toes." We're not going to say anything, we're just going to point. Here we go...

6. Now this time we will say ALL those things. Let's say, "Head." Let's say "Shoulders." Let's say "Knees," and let's say "Toes." Here we go...

Guess that smell!

1. Collect some strongly scented items and place them in a box so no one can see them.

2. Blindfold a child who has to smell one item at a time and try to guess what it is.

Item Suggestions:
Soap
Talcum Powder
Cut Lemon
Peppermint
Chocolate
Banana
Flowers

Ensure the child is not allergic to any of these items.

More Ideas!

You can try the same game with many options. For example, instead of "smell" you could try "taste," "feel," or "hear."

Have children trace around another child's body. They can then paint or color or use collage materials on their own outline. An adult can have small cards with the names of various body parts. As the adult reads the name of a body part, a child can put the label where it should go.

Limbo - Children walk forwards and bend back to get under a pole held by two people. The pole is lowered a little each time until only one child is able to get underneath it.

Wave scarves or ribbons while moving to music. Try different rhythms (marches, a waltz, skipping rhythm, etc.) and encourage the children to move to that rhythm.

Make an obstacle course with the help of the children. They can then go around it. Use words like "up," "down," "over," "under," "through."

Get Ready To Wiggle

(Murray Cook, Jeff Fatt, Anthony Field, Greg Page, John Field)
© 1991 Wiggly Tunes Pty. Ltd.
P.O. Box 657 Bondi Junction, NSW, 1355. AUSTRALIA.
International Copyright Secured. All Rights Reserved. Used by Permission.

Shuffle Feel

Intro:

Repeat x 4

A D7 A

D7 A D7 A

(Fine - 4th time)

Verse 1:   Get

A   D7   A   D7

read - y   to   wig - gle,   we've been read - y   for____ so   long____ get

A   D7   A   D7

read - y   to   wig - gle   when you wig - gle you can't____ go   wrong,____ get

A   D7   A   D7

read - y   to   wig - gle   wig - gle will make____ you   big and   strong____ get

A   D7   E7

read - y   to   wig - gle   c' - mon   wig - gle   to____ this   song,____

A   E7   A

—   wig - gle   to____ this   song.

Verse 2:
We're ready to wiggle, wiggle your fingers high in the sky,
We're ready to wiggle, wiggle your ears and wiggle your eyes,
We're ready to wiggle, wiggle your hair and wiggle your nose,
We're ready to wiggle, c'mon wiggle all ten toes,
Wiggle all ten toes.

Verse 3:
We can wiggle and wiggle, wiggle at home without a care,
Wiggle and wiggle, wiggle alone with your teddy bear,
Wiggle and wiggle, wiggle at breakfast, lunch and tea,
Wiggle and wiggle, wiggle along with me,
Wiggle along with me.

Make a Wiggly snake!

WHAT YOU NEED:
6 or more drink cans
Colored paper and/or
Material
Paint
Glue
String
Safety scissors

1. Paint the cans different colors and glue colored paper or pieces of material onto them.

2. Thread a length of string through as many decorated cans as you wish, stringing them loosely together with knots in-between each can.

3. Draw or paint two eyes and one long, red tongue on the paper or material. Cut out and glue these onto the first can.

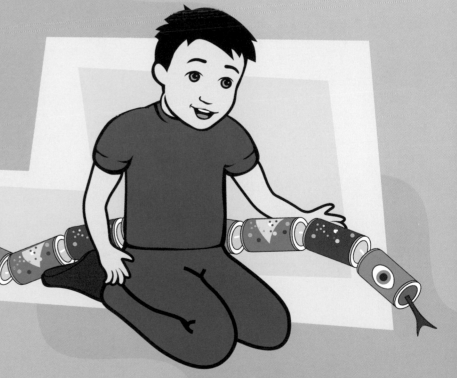

More Ideas!

Make a wiggly caterpillar from an egg carton:
Cut an egg carton down the middle, using six segments.
Paint it green and use pipe cleaners for antennae.
Paint black eyes and attach a cut-out
paper tongue if you wish.

Can You (Point Your Fingers & Do The Twist)?

(Murray Cook, Jeff Fatt, Anthony Field, Greg Page)
© 1995 Wiggly Tunes Pty. Ltd.
P.O. Box 657 Bondi Junction, NSW, 1355. AUSTRALIA.
International Copyright Secured. All Rights Reserved. Used by Permission.

Verse 1 & 3: Can you point ____ your__ fin - gers and do the twist?____ Can you point
Verse 2: on one foot____ and shake your hands?____ Can you stand

your____ fin - gers and do the__ twist?____ Well we're gon-na go
on one foot____ and shake your__ hands?____ Well we're gon-na go

up, then go down __ get back up and __ turn a - round.____ Can you point
up, then go down __ get back up and__ turn a - round.____ Can you stand

your ___ fin - gers and do the twist?____ Verse 2: Can you stand
on one foot____ and shake your hands?____

Making hand & footprints!

WHAT YOU NEED:
Paint
Large sheet of paper

1. Make handprints by painting the palms of your hands and pressing them onto a large sheet of paper.

2. Try it with your feet as well!

More Ideas!

Extend the song
"Can You (Paint Your Fingers And Do The Twist)?"
by getting the children to think of other
pairs of actions they can do.

Move Your Arms Like Henry

(Paul Field)
© 1998 Wiggly Tunes Pty. Ltd.
P.O. Box 657 Bondi Junction, NSW, 1355. AUSTRALIA.
International Copyright Secured. All Rights Reserved. Used by Permission.

Chorus: G

(no repeat on D.S.)

Move your arms, ___ like Hen - ry.
- ry, Shake your hands ___ like Hen -

D

Move your arms ___ like Hen -
ry.
ry.

Move your arms ___ a - round, and a - round, and a -
Shake your hands ___ a - round, and a - round, and a -

C   G

*Fine
on D.S.*

round and a - round ___ like Hen - ry.
round and a - round ___ like Hen - ry.

Shake your hands ___ like Hen -

Verse: C   G

Hen - ry waves to you. ___

Hen - ry waves to me. ___

D7

D.S. no repeat

He's got so man - y hands he's wav - ing ___ all the time. ___

26

Make an octopus!

1. Partially inflate a balloon (about three quarters full).

2. Glue or tape EIGHT strips onto the balloon.

GLUE

3. Using paint or markers, make two eyes and a mouth on the balloon and your octopus is ready!

PAINT

More Ideas!

Have a container with water in it and give each child a small object. Each child has to guess whether his or her object will float or sink. Have them give a reason for their suggestions, then check their assumptions.

Use a small carton and make a sea diorama. Paint the inside of the carton blue/green and add shells, small rocks, sand, or other objects that have been collected. Fish can be cut from cardboard using saftey scissors and hung from the top of the box.

Make shell patterns in play dough.

Rock-A-Bye Your Bear

(Murray Cook, Jeff Fatt, Anthony Field, Greg Page)
© 1991 Wiggly Tunes Pty. Ltd.
P.O. Box 657 Bondi Junction, NSW, 1355. AUSTRALIA.
International Copyright Secured. All Rights Reserved. Used by Permission.

28

Make a bear's head!

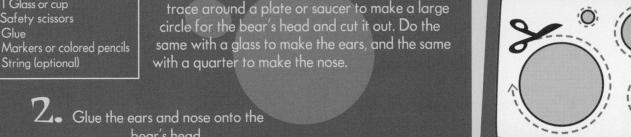

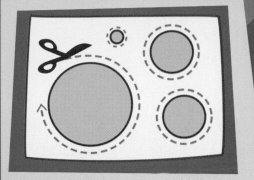

WHAT YOU NEED:
Cardboard or paper
1 Kitchen plate or saucer
1 Glass or cup
Safety scissors
Glue
Markers or colored pencils
String (optional)

1. Using either cardboard or paper, trace around a plate or saucer to make a large circle for the bear's head and cut it out. Do the same with a glass to make the ears, and the same with a quarter to make the nose.

2. Glue the ears and nose onto the bear's head.

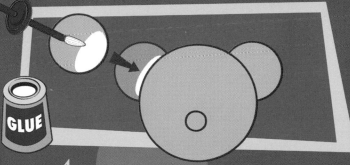

3. Color or paint your bear, making sure to include the eyes, mouth and fur!

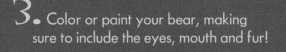

4. When you are finished, you can thread some string through the top of the bear's head and hang it up.

More Ideas!

Talk with the children about different kinds of bears, where they live and what they eat.

Wiggly Party

(Murray Cook, Jeff Fatt, Anthony Field, Greg Page, John Field, Craig Abercrombie)
© 2001 Wiggly Tunes Pty. Ltd.
P.O. Box 657 Bondi Junction, NSW, 1355. AUSTRALIA.
International Copyright Secured. All Rights Reserved. Used by Permission.

Chorus:

Wig-gl-y par - ty, (eve-ry-bod-y's com-ing), Wig-gl-y par - ty, (eve-ry-bod-y's com-ing),

Wig-gl-y par - ty, (eve-ry-bod-y's com-ing), stamp, stamp, stamp, clap, clap, clap, Wig-gle your hips, just like that!

Verse:

Pin the tail____ on ____ the don-key, now we're play-ing hide____ and seek,____
Put on your par-ty____ hats,____ and your dress up cos - tumes too.____

Repeat x3

and in the kitch - en____ we're mak-ing, all the fruit sal - ad you can eat.____ At the
Pass__ the par - cel__ and then,__ there's a pres-ent for me and you.____ At the

Make a Wiggly Party hat!

1. Cut out a cone-shaped piece of cardboard and decorate it using markers or colored pencils.

2. Glue or staple the sides of the cardboard together. Trim to fit and attach a thin piece of elastic to go under the child's chin to help keep it on.

More Ideas!

Make a piñata. Fill up a balloon with dried fruit. Blow up the balloon and have the children cover it with finely shredded pieces of newspaper and plenty of paste. Leave it to dry. The children take turns to hit the piñata and burst it and catch the dried fruit as it falls out.

Make streamers. Children can make streamers from colored paper. Make blue, yellow, red and purple chains and join them to make a long chain.

Folding paper chains. Cut long strips of colored paper or use ordinary streamers. Glue the ends at right angles and then fold one piece over the other. Talk about the angles and shapes as you go.

Pin the tail on the dinosaur. Have a big outline picture of Dorothy The Dinosaur. Children can color it green with yellow spots. Make several tails and play "Pin The Tail On The Dinosaur."

Make some party food:
*Fruit Kebabs made by threading strawberries, apple pieces, seedless grapes and other pieces of fruit onto a fine satay stick.
* Fruit Salad
* Make a cheese and tomato hedgehog by threading a cherry tomato and a small square of cheese onto a toothpick. Stick the toothpicks into an orange.
* Milkshakes
* Fruit juice cubes. Pour some fruit juice into an ice cube tray.

The Monkey Dance

(Murray Cook, Jeff Fatt, Anthony Field, Greg Page, John Field)
© 1994 Wiggly Tunes Pty. Ltd.
P.O. Box 657 Bondi Junction, NSW, 1355. AUSTRALIA.
International Copyright Secured. All Rights Reserved. Used by Permission.

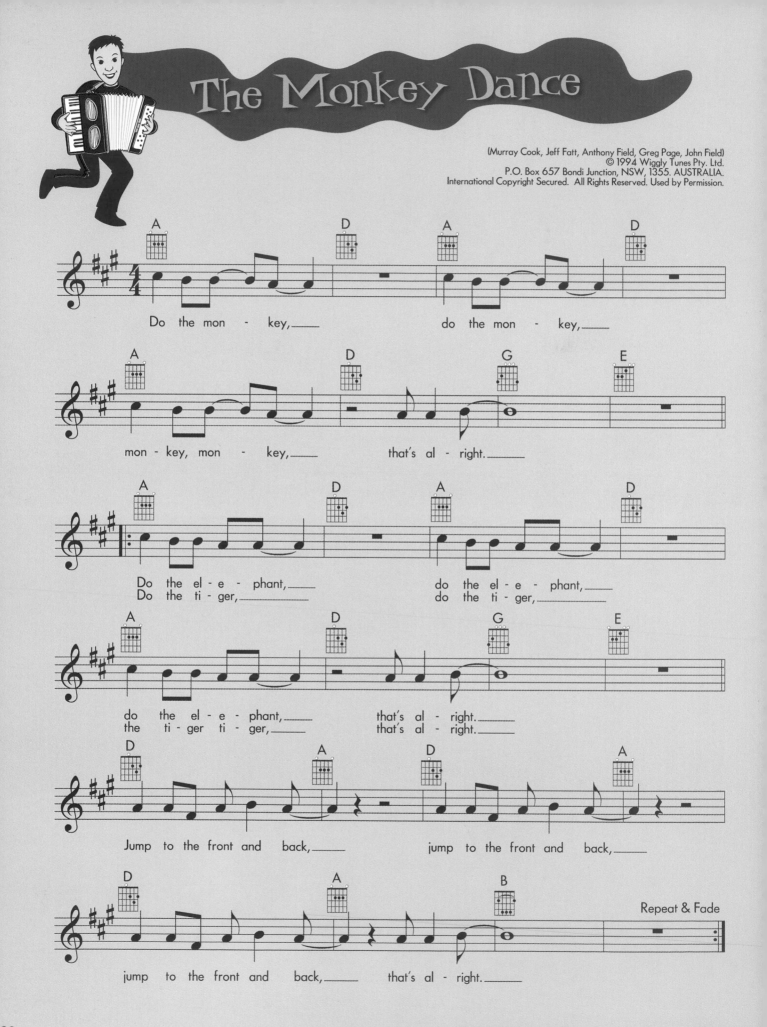

Do the mon - key,_____ do the mon - key,_____

mon - key, mon - key,_____ that's al - right._____

Do the el - e - phant,_____ do the el - e - phant,_____
Do the ti - ger,_____ do the ti - ger,_____

do the el - e - phant,_____ that's al - right._____
the ti - ger ti - ger,_____ that's al - right._____

Jump to the front and back,_____ jump to the front and back,_____

Repeat & Fade

jump to the front and back,_____ that's al - right._____

Making binoculars!

1. Paint the toilet paper rolls any color you like.

2. Glue the two rolls together in the shape of a pair of binoculars.

3. Pierce a hole in one end of each of the rolls and thread a piece of string through so that you can hang the binoculars around your neck. Then see if you can spot some animals in the jungle!

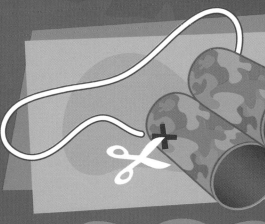

More Ideas!

Visit a zoo.

Look at pictures of jungle animals and talk about them with the children.

Make some trees for the jungle. Roll three sheets of newspaper, overlapping them as you roll. Tape the bottom of the roll and make four or five deep cuts through the rolled paper to about one-third of the way down from the top. Gently pull the "leaves" out from the middle of the roll. Use green and brown paint to paint the tree.

Do The Owl

(Murray Cook, Jeff Fatt, Anthony Field, Greg Page, John Field, Dominic Lindsay, Steve Irwin)
© 2002 Wiggly Tunes Pty. Ltd.
P.O. Box 657 Bondi Junction, NSW, 1355. AUSTRALIA.
International Copyright Secured. All Rights Reserved. Used by Permission.

Chorus: D7 ... G7

Hoo - hoo,_____ Hoo - hoo,_____ Do The Owl!_____

D7 ... G7

Hoo - hoo,_____ Hoo - hoo,_____ Do The Owl!

Verse: Bm ... G7

The owl is a type_____ of ____ bird,____ found all a - round____ the ____ world.____
They come out by the light of the moon,___ that's when they____ find_____ their ____food,____
They live in a cave ____ or ____ tree,____ they use their great big eyes to ___ see,____

Bm ... G7

Get your hands and make big_____ owl____ eyes,_____ we're gon-na Do The___Owl.
So ___ spread your si - lent___wings,_____ we're gon-na Do The___Owl.
Fly - ing from tree____ to ____ tree,_____ we're gon-na Do The___Owl.

Repeat x 3

Chorus: D7 ... G7

Hoo - hoo,_____ Hoo - hoo,_____ Do The Owl!_____

D7 ... G7

Repeat & Fade

Hoo - hoo,_____ Hoo - hoo,_____ Do The Owl!

Make your own owl!

1. Draw the outline of an owl's head and body onto a large piece of paper or cardboard and cut out.

2. Paint the owl using brown, gray, or white paint depending on the type of owl you are making.

4. Paint a beak or make one from cardboard or paper and glue it on.

3. Cut individual egg holders from an egg carton and paint them for the owl's eyes. Attach with glue.

More Ideas!

Show children pictures of the different varieties of owls. Talk about where they live and what they eat.

Discuss nocturnal animals and birds, including owls.

Move Like An Emu

(Murray Cook, Jeff Fatt, Anthony Field, Greg Page, John Field)
© 2001 Wiggly Tunes Pty. Ltd.
P.O. Box 657 Bondi Junction, NSW, 1355. AUSTRALIA.
International Copyright Secured. All Rights Reserved. Used by Permission.

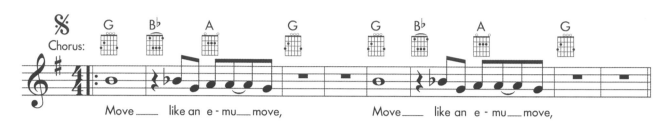

Chorus:
Move ___ like an e-mu ___ move, Move ___ like an e-mu ___ move,

1. & 3.
Verse:
Put your hand up, in the ___ air, ___ just like an e-mu.

To CODA on 3rd time

Make a beak, to peck eve-ry-where, peck eve-ry-where that's what we do when we mo-

2. (breakdown)
Stretch out ___ your long legs. Scratch with ___ your feet. Fluff out ___ your feath-ers.

D.S. al Coda

Beak goes up, beak goes down, beak goes peck-ing all a-round, shake your wings and run around, Oh Oh Oh!

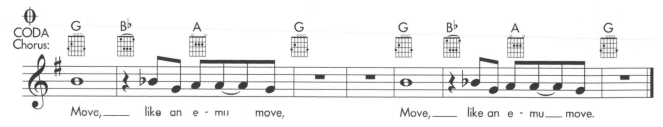

CODA
Chorus:
Move, ___ like an e-mu move, Move, ___ like an e-mu move.

Attaching feathers to your emu!

WHAT YOU NEED:
Safety scissors
1 Large sheet of paper
Glue
Any 1 of the following:
Brown paper
Brown crayons
Brown paint

1. Draw an emu on a large piece of paper.

2. Paper feathers can be made by folding curved, triangular pieces of brown paper in half and then cutting towards the fold. Use crayons or paint to color them. Strips of brown crepe paper could also be used as feathers.

More Ideas!

Visit a wildlife park.

Show pictures of ostriches and emus and discuss the differences between them.

Play the game **Emu/Ostrich**
All children sit in a circle. One child goes around the circle and touches each child on the shoulder saying, "Emu," to each one. Then he or she says, "Ostrich!"
The child patted when "Ostrich!" is spoken must get up and chase the first child around the ring until he/she comes back to that place.
Then the second child goes around the ring, patting the other children.

Henry's Underwater Big Band

(John Field)
© 1996 Wiggly Tunes Pty. Ltd.
P.O. Box 657 Bondi Junction, NSW, 1355. AUSTRALIA.
International Copyright Secured. All Rights Reserved. Used by Permission.

Verse:

Eve-ry night___ un-der the sea,___ the friend-ly oc-to-pus Hen-ry, leads his

Chorus:

Un-der-wa - ter An - i-mal___ Big Band. Henry: (Now Jellyfish, you play the drums, Walruses, you can hum. Electric Eel, why don't you play your guitar?) So clap your hands,

with Hen - ry,___ turn a-round___ and shout YIP-EE! 'Cause his un - der-wa-ter band___ is now read-y.___

1. 2.

Eve - ry-bod-y shout Hip Hip Hoo - ray!___ When Hen-ry's Big Band___ be-gins to play.

Repeat x 3

3.

Big Band___ be - gins to Big Band___ be -gins to Big Band___ be - gins to play.___

Verse 2:
Spoken:
Now dolphins play the trumpet loud,
You're sure to bring a crowd,
Seahorse you can play the glockenspiel,
The tortoise shell is timpani,
It's lots of fun for you and me.
Sing:
Henry's Underwater Animal Big Band!

Make your own seashell mobile!

WHAT YOU NEED:
Seashells
Glue
String
Small sticks or
wire coat hanger

1. Visit the seaside and collect some shells.

2. Attach the seashells to pieces of string and attach these to either a stick or a wire coat hanger. Hang above a window.

More Ideas!

Use a small carton and make a sea diorama. Paint the inside of the carton blue/green and add the shells, small rocks, sand, or other objects that have been collected. Fish can be cut from cardboard and hung from the top of the box.

Make some musical instruments like tapping sticks or shakers with different things inside (such as small shells, sand, or pebbles) and glass bottles with different levels of water in them and have your own band.